Sainsbury's

·RECIPE·LIBRARY·

MICROWAVE COOKING

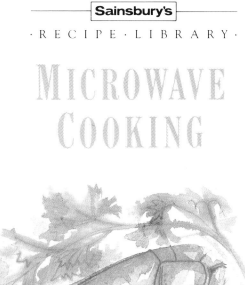
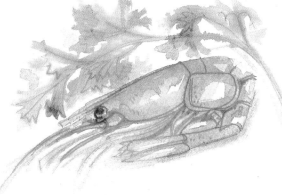

TIMER

0 2 4 6 8 10 12 14 16 18 20 22 24 26 28 30

COOK CONTROL

MED
MED HIGH
MED LOW
DEFROST
HIGH
LOW

HIGH
Bacon (2 back rashers)   7 oz (200g)   1 1/2 min.
Beefburgers (frozen)   1 lb (450g)   4 1/2 min.
Fish Fillets   5 min.

MED LOW / DEFROST
Frozen Small Sliced Loaf   4 1/2 min.
Frozen Lamb Chops   1 lb (450g)   7 1/2 min.

OPEN DOOR

START

R-6261 MADE IN JAPAN

Sainsbury's
·RECIPE·LIBRARY·

MICROWAVE COOKING

Lorna Rhodes

CONTENTS

Published exclusively for J Sainsbury plc
Stamford House Stamford Street
London SE1 9LL
by Woodhead-Faulkner Ltd
Fitzwilliam House 32 Trumpington Street
Cambridge CB2 1QY

INTRODUCTION

If you already own a microwave oven and have followed the basic cooking methods given in the manufacturer's handbook, you will have discovered all the advantages of microwave cooking. It defrosts and cooks quickly, reheats without drying the food, and creates less washing-up. It is clean to use, convenient to place in the kitchen, but most of all it cooks many foods perfectly, retaining the flavours and texture of foods such as fish and vegetables and minimizing the loss of nutrients which often occurs in other cooking methods.

More and more people are being attracted to microwave cooking, particularly those who do not like spending time in the kitchen, and those who enjoy cooking but have not got the time. Microwave ovens are so easy to use and so much safer than a conventional oven that they are ideal for older people who may only cook small amounts of food and for the disabled who can site the cooker at a comfortable level. There are also considerable savings in fuel consumption because meals can be produced in only a quarter or fifth of the normal cooking time and the microwave oven uses less power than a conventional oven. The kitchen stays cooler and windows do not get steamed up.

RECIPE GUIDELINES

The recipes in this book will show you just how versatile microwave cooking can be. Tables giving defrosting and cooking times for individual food items are not given as these will be found in your handbooks. Most of the cooking methods suitable for a microwave are used in the recipes, and the variety of dishes will be sure to please both family and friends.

The wattage of your microwave oven will determine how long food takes to cook. All these recipes have been tested on a 650 watt microwave oven with a turntable. For a 500 watt microwave oven increase the cooking time by about 40 seconds for every minute given and for a 600 watt oven increase the cooking time by 20 seconds per minute.

Most microwave ovens now have a variable power control which may be described as HIGH, MEDIUM and LOW; or may be referred to as FULL POWER, ROAST, SIMMER, DEFROST and WARM; or it could be described as % of full power. Whichever control your oven has, the highest setting will be equivalent to FULL POWER or 100% energy output.

FULL POWER is used for most general high-speed cooking methods, for instance when cooking fish, vegetables, fruits, hot drinks, bacon, preheating the browning dish and melting butter. It is the *only* setting available on basic on/off microwave models.

MEDIUM POWER is used primarily for baking, roasting, cooking casseroles and for reheating previously cooked foods. Foods retain more moisture on MEDIUM, and reducing the power means less stirring and watching.

LOW POWER is used for defrosting and simmering, softening butter and it is the setting used for very gentle cooking.

A GUIDE TO COMPARATIVE CONTROL SETTINGS

Descriptions used in this book	HIGH	MEDIUM	LOW	DEFROST
Other comparable descriptions used	FULL	ROAST BAKE	SIMMER STEW	DEFROST
	7	6–5	4–3	2
APPROXIMATE POWER OUTPUT	100%	50%–60%	30%	20%

TIMING

Timing is very important in microwave cooking—overcooking will dry out the food and make it tough. It is always better to undercook the food, as it can be returned to the oven for a while longer if necessary. Microwave models vary greatly, so to ensure you do not overcook food, check it well before due time.

As the food is cooked so quickly, it will retain a great deal of heat after it has been taken out of the oven and will continue to cook. This has been taken into account in the recipes and is another reason why it is most important to observe the times.

If a standing time is given in a recipe, cover the food with foil when it is removed from the oven and leave to stand for the time indicated. If for any reason after this period the food requires additional microwave time, it can be cooked a little longer, but the standing time does not need to be repeated.

The times given in these recipes are specific to the quantity of the food being cooked. If you alter the amounts given in the recipes, the cooking time will need to be adapted. In general, when doubling the amount of food, increase the cooking time by one third to one half.

When planning to cook a whole meal in your microwave oven, remember that most meat, fish and poultry dishes improve upon standing and can be reheated quickly. Those foods which require standing time should therefore be cooked first, and quick-cooking dishes cooked during that standing time.

COOKING EQUIPMENT

For general all-round use, glass, pottery and china can be used in the microwave; check that the dishes do not have a metallic rim.

For shorter cooking periods, paper cookware, greaseproof paper, kitchen paper and cardboard can be used. Plastic is ideal for short cooking times, as are cooking and roasting bags.

Special microwave equipment is available, such as defrost boxes, microwave thermometers (specially made without mercury), and various shaped cookware made in durable plastic. Browning skillets have a special non-stick coating which absorbs microwave energy. When preheated, the skillets become hot and can then be used to brown and seal chops, chicken portions and joints of meat prior to roasting.

COVERING FOOD

Whenever a recipe states 'cover', use either the lids provided with the microwave containers or clingfilm placed over the dish. If using clingfilm, pierce it in two places with a small sharp knife to allow steam to escape and so prevent ballooning.

HELPFUL HINTS

- Always use ovengloves to remove dishes from the microwave oven as they can be quite hot.
- Do not overload the oven, or its speed and efficiency will be impaired.
- For foods that should contain moisture, always cover food when cooking on HIGH. The cover should not be completely airtight for long cooking times: stretch the clingfilm over the dish and then fold back one corner.
- After cooking, peel back the clingfilm from the far side of the dish to avoid steam burns.
- Use the oven to freshen up stale coffee beans.
- Soak 1 sachet gelatine in water until spongy, then microwave on HIGH for 1 minute or until clear.
- Place herbs and citrus rinds on a plate and microwave on HIGH until dry. Cool and store in containers.
- Microwave butter on LOW for 1 minute to soften.
- Prick the skins of citrus fruits and microwave on HIGH for 10 seconds to gain maximum juice when squeezed.
- Break chocolate into a bowl and microwave on MEDIUM for 1 minute per 25 g (1 oz) to melt.
- Microwave nuts on HIGH for 4–5 minutes, until lightly brown, stirring twice.

NOTES

Ingredients are given in both metric and imperial measures. Use either set of quantities but not a mixture of both in any one recipe.

All spoon measurements are level:
1 tablespoon = one 15 ml spoon
1 teaspoon = one 5 ml spoon.

All recipes have been tested on 650 watt microwave ovens. Models with different power levels can be used by making adjustments to cooking times (see page 5).

Freshly ground black pepper is intended where pepper is listed.

Fresh herbs are used unless otherwise stated. If unobtainable dried herbs can be substituted in cooked dishes but halve the quantities.

Eggs are standard size 3 unless otherwise stated.

Always follow your microwave oven manufacturer's operating instructions and recommendations.

CURRIED PARSNIP SOUP

25 g (1 oz) butter or
    margarine
1 small onion, chopped
500 g (1 lb) parsnips, sliced
    thinly

2 teaspoons mild curry
    powder
1 litre (1¾ pints) hot
    chicken stock
salt and pepper to taste
snipped chives to garnish

Serves 4
Preparation time:
10 minutes
Power setting:
HIGH
Cooking time:
21 minutes

1. Place the butter or margarine in a large bowl and microwave on HIGH for 1 minute. Add the onion and parsnips, then cover and cook on HIGH for 3 minutes.
2. Stir in the curry powder and cook on HIGH for 2 minutes.
3. Pour in the stock, season with salt and pepper, then cover and cook on HIGH for 15 minutes or until the parsnips are tender.
4. Put the soup into a blender or food processor and work until smooth. Garnish with snipped chives and serve immediately, with crusty bread.

TOMATO AND CARROT SOUP

25 g (1 oz) butter
1 onion, chopped
250 g (8 oz) carrots, sliced
    thinly
500 g (1 lb) ripe tomatoes,
    skinned and chopped
1 teaspoon sugar

600 ml (1 pint) hot
    vegetable stock
rosemary sprig
salt and pepper to taste
flat-leaved parsley to
    garnish

Serves 4
Preparation time:
15 minutes
Power setting:
HIGH
Cooking time:
26 minutes

1. Place the butter in a large bowl and microwave on HIGH for 1 minute. Add the onion and carrots and cook for 5 minutes.
2. Add the tomatoes, sugar, stock and rosemary to the bowl, cover and cook on HIGH for 18 minutes.
3. Remove the rosemary, then pour the soup into a blender or food processor and work until smooth. Season with salt and pepper, then return to the bowl and cook on HIGH for 2 minutes.
4. Garnish with parsley to serve.

CREAMY WATERCRESS SOUP

This fresh-tasting soup can be served chilled for a summer meal or hot with croûtons.

50 g (2 oz) butter
2 large bunches watercress, chopped
1 onion, chopped
600 ml (1 pint) hot vegetable stock

1 teaspoon lemon juice
25 g (1 oz) cornflour
300 ml (½ pint) milk
pinch of grated nutmeg
salt and pepper to taste
4 tablespoons single cream

Serves 4
Preparation time: 10 minutes
Power setting: HIGH
Cooking time: 16 minutes

1. Place the butter in a large bowl and microwave on HIGH for 1 minute. Add the watercress and onion, cover the bowl and cook for 5 minutes.
2. Add the stock, lemon juice, and salt and pepper, cover the bowl and cook on HIGH for 5 minutes.
3. Cool a little, then pour into a blender or food processor and work until smooth.
4. Blend the cornflour with a little of the milk to a smooth paste, then stir in the remaining milk and the nutmeg. Add to the soup, return to the bowl, cover and cook on HIGH for 5 minutes.
5. Serve with a swirl of cream on each portion of soup.

CORN AND CHICKEN CHOWDER

25 g (1 oz) butter
1 onion, chopped
250 g (8 oz) potato, diced
2 tablespoons plain flour
1/4 teaspoon turmeric
600 ml (1 pint) hot chicken stock

326 g (11 1/2 oz) can sweetcorn kernels, drained
170 g (6 oz) can evaporated milk
175 g (6 oz) cooked chicken, diced
salt and pepper to taste
chopped parsley to garnish

1. Place the butter in a bowl and microwave on HIGH for 1 minute. Add the onion and potato and cook for 3 minutes.
2. Stir in the flour and turmeric, then blend in the chicken stock. Add two thirds of the sweetcorn, cover and cook on HIGH for 15 minutes.
3. Stir in the evaporated milk, then pour the soup into a blender or food processor; work until almost smooth.
4. Return to the bowl, add the chicken, reserved sweetcorn, and salt and pepper. Cover and cook on HIGH for 3 minutes. Serve garnished with chopped parsley.

Serves 4
Preparation time:
10 minutes
Power setting:
HIGH
Cooking time:
22 minutes

FRENCH-STYLE PÂTÉ

6–8 rashers streaky bacon, derinded	1 clove garlic, crushed
25 g (1 oz) butter	3 tablespoons sherry
250 g (8 oz) chicken livers, chopped	1 teaspoon chopped mixed herbs
250 g (8 oz) minced pork	pinch of grated nutmeg
125 g (4 oz) sausagemeat	salt and pepper to taste
	2–3 bay leaves

Serves 4–6
Preparation time: 15 minutes, plus chilling time
Power setting: HIGH
Cooking time: 10 minutes

1. Lay the bacon rashers flat on a board and stretch with the back of a knife; use half to line a 500 g (1 lb) microwave loaf tin or earthenware terrine.
2. Combine the butter, livers, pork and sausagemeat in a bowl. Cover and cook on HIGH for 6 minutes or until the meat is cooked, stirring twice during cooking.
3. Place the mixture in a blender or food processor, add the garlic, sherry, herbs, nutmeg, and salt and pepper and work until smooth.
4. Spoon the mixture into the prepared tin and cover with the remaining bacon. Place 2 or 3 bay leaves on top. Cover with clingfilm and cook on HIGH for 4 minutes.
5. Leave to cool, then cover with foil, weight down and chill overnight.
6. Turn out onto a serving plate and slice. Serve with French bread and a green salad.

MINESTRONE

A nourishing Italian vegetable soup, minestrone makes a hearty meal served with crisp rolls and butter. The vegetables used in this recipe can be varied, with the addition of cooked dried beans if you like.

4 tablespoons olive oil	125 g (4 oz) Savoy cabbage, shredded
2 rashers streaky bacon, derinded and chopped	3 tablespoons tomato purée
1 onion, chopped	25 g (1 oz) small pasta shapes
1 clove garlic, crushed	900 ml (1½ pints) hot chicken stock
2 celery sticks, sliced	salt and pepper to taste
2 carrots, diced	freshly grated Parmesan cheese to serve
1 potato, diced	
75 g (3 oz) French beans	
2 courgettes, diced	
3 ripe tomatoes, skinned, seeded and chopped	

1. Place the oil, bacon, onion, garlic and celery in a large bowl and cook on HIGH for 5 minutes.
2. Add the carrots and potato, cover and cook on HIGH for 5 minutes, stirring once or twice.
3. Cut the French beans into 2.5 cm (1 inch) lengths and add to the bowl with the courgettes. Cover and cook on HIGH for 2 minutes. Stir in the tomatoes, cabbage, tomato purée and pasta.
4. Add the hot chicken stock to the bowl, and season with salt and pepper. Cover the bowl and cook on HIGH for 10 minutes.
5. Serve in warmed individual soup bowls, with Parmesan cheese handed separately.

Serves 4–6
Preparation time:
15 minutes
Power setting:
HIGH
Cooking time:
22 minutes

GINGER PRAWNS

Serves 4
Preparation time:
10 minutes
Power setting:
HIGH
Cooking time:
2 minutes

250 g (8 oz) peeled prawns
250 g (8 oz) bean sprouts
3 spring onions, shredded
½ red pepper, sliced finely

1 teaspoon finely chopped
  fresh root ginger
2 teaspoons oyster sauce
2 teaspoons sesame oil
1 tablespoon soy sauce

Place all the ingredients in a large bowl, then cook on HIGH for 2 minutes. Stir and serve immediately.

MUSHROOM PÂTÉ

40 g (1½ oz) butter
1 small onion, chopped
250 g (8 oz) flat
  mushrooms
113 g (4 oz) cream cheese

25 g (1 oz) fresh
  breadcrumbs
1 tablespoon mushroom
  ketchup
salt and pepper to taste

Serves 4
Preparation time:
10 minutes, plus
chilling time
Power setting:
HIGH
Cooking time:
6½ minutes

1. Place the butter in a bowl and microwave on HIGH for 30 seconds. Add the onion and cook for 2 minutes.
2. Chop the mushrooms finely, then squeeze them in kitchen paper to remove excess liquid. Add to the onion and cook on HIGH for 4 minutes. Drain well.
3. Transfer the mixture to a blender or food processor, add the remaining ingredients and work to a rough purée.
4. Spoon the pâté into a serving dish, cover and chill for at least 4 hours or overnight. Serve with Melba toast.

DEVILLED CORN ON THE COB

75 g (3 oz) butter
3 tablespoons tomato
  ketchup

2 teaspoons Worcestershire
  sauce
1 teaspoon Dijon mustard
4 corn cobs

Serves 4
Preparation time:
5 minutes
Power setting:
HIGH
Cooking time:
12–15 minutes

1. Soften the butter in the microwave on HIGH for 30 seconds, then blend in the tomato ketchup, Worcestershire sauce and mustard.
2. Place each corn cob on a piece of greaseproof paper and spread with the butter mixture. Wrap the cobs in the paper, and place in a large dish in a single layer.
3. Cook on HIGH until tender—about 12 minutes if fresh or 15 minutes if frozen; turn halfway through cooking.
4. Serve the corn with the buttery juices poured over.

CHICKEN TERIYAKI KEBABS

With its authentic Japanese flavour, this is a succulent and impressive way to serve chicken as a starter. To make spring onion tassels for the garnish, trim the onions and cut the green part into fine strips. Place in a bowl of iced water and leave to stand for about 30 minutes; drain on kitchen paper.

2 boneless chicken breasts, skinned
2 tablespoons soy sauce
1 teaspoon demerara sugar
2 tablespoons dry sherry
1 teaspoon finely chopped fresh root ginger

1 clove garlic, crushed
oil for brushing
TO GARNISH:
shredded lettuce
4 spring onion tassels (see above)

Serves 4
Preparation time:
15 minutes, plus marinating
Power setting:
HIGH
Cooking time:
6 minutes

1. Cut the chicken into small pieces and place in a dish.
2. Combine the soy sauce, sugar, sherry, ginger and garlic, pour over the chicken and mix together. Cover and chill overnight.
3. Thread the chicken onto 8 wooden cocktail sticks. Place on a microwave rack over a dish, brush with oil and cook on HIGH for 6 minutes, turning halfway through cooking.
4. Serve hot, on a bed of shredded lettuce, garnished with the spring onion tassels.

PRAWNS PROVENÇALE

500 g (1 lb) ripe tomatoes, skinned, seeded and chopped
1 tablespoon olive oil
1 small onion, chopped finely
1 clove garlic, crushed

1 teaspoon chopped basil
1 tablespoon tomato purée
250 g (8 oz) peeled prawns
1 tablespoon chopped red pepper
salt and pepper to taste
basil leaves to garnish

Serves 4
Preparation time:
10 minutes
Power setting:
HIGH
Cooking time:
13 minutes

1. Place the tomato flesh in a bowl with the oil, onion, garlic, basil, and salt and pepper. Cover and cook on HIGH for 10 minutes, stirring twice during cooking.
2. Place in a blender or food processor and work until smooth. Return to the bowl, stir in the remaining ingredients, cover and cook on HIGH for 3 minutes.
3. Spoon into individual dishes and garnish with basil. Serve with crusty French bread.

STILTON MUSHROOMS

250 g (8 oz) large flat
mushrooms
50 g (2 oz) butter
2 shallots, chopped finely

175 g (6 oz) Stilton cheese
25 g (1 oz) fresh
breadcrumbs
salt and pepper to taste

1. Carefully remove the stalks from the mushrooms and chop finely. Wipe the caps with damp kitchen paper.
2. Place half of the butter in a bowl and microwave on HIGH for 1 minute, then add the mushroom stalks and shallots and cook on HIGH for 2 minutes.
3. Leave to cool for 5 minutes, then crumble in the cheese, add the breadcrumbs, and salt and pepper and mix well. Divide the mixture between the mushroom caps.
4. Place the remaining butter in a large shallow dish and microwave on HIGH for 1 minute. Place the stuffed mushrooms in the dish and cook for 2 minutes.
5. Serve immediately.

Serves 4
Preparation time:
15 minutes
Power setting:
HIGH
Cooking time:
6 minutes

AVOCADO AND CRAB THERMIDOR

15 g (½ oz) butter
2 tablespoons plain flour
150 ml (¼ pint) milk
1 teaspoon tomato purée
juice of ½ lemon
good pinch of cayenne
* pepper*

250 g (8 oz) crabmeat,
* fresh, frozen or canned*
2 large avocados, halved
* and stoned*
4 teaspoons grated
* Parmesan cheese*
salt and pepper to taste

Serves 4
Preparation time:
10 minutes
Power setting:
HIGH
Cooking time:
7 minutes

1. Place the butter in a small bowl and microwave on HIGH for 30 seconds. Stir in the flour and return to the microwave for 30 seconds.
2. Pour the milk into a jug and heat on HIGH for 1 minute, then gradually blend into the butter and flour. Cook on HIGH for 2 minutes, whisking every 30 seconds.
3. Add the tomato purée, 1 teaspoon of the lemon juice, cayenne, and salt and pepper to the sauce, then stir in the crabmeat.
4. Sprinkle the avocado flesh with remaining lemon juice.
5. Pile the crabmeat filling into the avocado halves, then sprinkle with the Parmesan cheese. Place in a shallow dish and cook on HIGH for 3 minutes. Serve hot, with brown bread and butter.

HOT ANCHOVY DIP

This Italian dish, known as *Bagna Cauda*, is served as a hot dip for raw vegetables. It is ideal as a first course for a dinner party. If a small spirit burner is available, place the dip in a fondue dish over the burner to keep hot.

50 g (2 oz) butter
4 tablespoons olive oil
2 cloves garlic, chopped
50 g (1¾ oz) can
* anchovies, drained*

TO SERVE:
variety of vegetables (e.g.
* celery, carrot,*
* cucumber, green or red*
* pepper), cut into strips*

Serves 4
Preparation time:
10 minutes
Power setting:
HIGH and
MEDIUM
Cooking time:
5 minutes

1. Place the butter and oil in a bowl and microwave on HIGH for 2 minutes. Add the garlic and cook for 1 minute.
2. Chop the anchovies, add them to the bowl, cover and cook on MEDIUM for 2 minutes.
3. Carefully transfer the mixture to a blender or food processor and work until smooth. Pour the dip into a warmed serving bowl, place on a large plate and surround with the vegetables. Serve immediately.

MAIN COURSES

PLAICE ROLLS WITH CAPER SAUCE

8 plaice fillets, skinned
4 tablespoons dry white
  wine
1 tablespoon lemon juice
2 egg yolks

5 tablespoons double
  cream
2 teaspoons capers
salt and pepper to taste

Serves 4
Preparation time:
15 minutes
Power setting:
HIGH
Cooking time:
7½ minutes

1. Roll up the plaice fillets and arrange in a shallow dish in a single layer. Mix together the wine and lemon juice, season with salt and pepper, then sprinkle over the fish. Cover and cook on HIGH for 5 minutes.
2. Using a slotted spoon, transfer the plaice rolls to a warmed serving dish and cover with foil to keep warm. Reserve the fish liquor.
3. Beat the egg yolks and cream together in a small bowl, then stir into the fish liquor. Add the capers, then cook on HIGH for 2½ minutes, stirring every 30 seconds.
4. Pour the sauce over the fish and serve immediately.

SPANISH FISH PARCELS

750 g (1½ lb) coley, cod or
  haddock fillet, cut into
  4 pieces
1 tablespoon olive oil
½ each red and green
  pepper, cored, seeded
  and chopped
4 spring onions, chopped

2 large tomatoes, skinned,
  seeded and chopped
2 celery sticks, chopped
1 clove garlic, crushed
salt and pepper to taste
flat-leaved parsley to
  garnish

Serves 4
Preparation time:
20 minutes
Power setting:
HIGH
Cooking time:
10 minutes

1. Place each piece of fish on a large piece of greaseproof paper.
2. Mix the remaining ingredients together in a bowl, cover and cook on HIGH for 3 minutes. Divide between the fish.
3. Wrap each piece of fish in its paper to make a parcel. Place in a dish and cook on HIGH for 7 minutes.
4. Unwrap each parcel and carefully lift the fish onto a warmed serving plate. Spoon the vegetables on top. Garnish with flat-leaved parsley to serve.

SRI LANKAN FISH

This quick curry is easy to prepare. The coconut and pineapple lend a delicate flavour to the fish and the subtle blend of spices gives a truly authentic taste.

1 onion, sliced
750 g (1½ lb) thick
  haddock or cod fillet,
  skinned and cut into
  7.5 cm (3 inch) pieces
3 dried red chillies, soaked
  for 10 minutes
75 g (3 oz) creamed
  coconut, blended with
  150 ml (¼ pint) hot
  water
½ teaspoon ground
  cumin
½ teaspoon turmeric
½ teaspoon ground
  fenugreek

pinch of ground
  cinnamon
1 tablespoon ground
  coriander
1 teaspoon finely grated
  fresh root ginger
1 teaspoon finely grated
  lemon rind
2 tablespoons lemon juice
227 g (8 oz) can pineapple
  pieces in natural juice
1 tablespoon cornflour,
  blended with
  2 tablespoons milk
salt and pepper to taste

Serves 4
Preparation time:
20 minutes
Power setting:
HIGH
Cooking time:
11 minutes

1. Place the onion in a large shallow dish, cover and cook on HIGH for 2 minutes. Lay the fish on top.
2. Seed and chop the chillies, then sprinkle over the fish.
3. Place the coconut milk, spices, grated ginger, and lemon rind and juice in a blender or food processor. Add the pineapple and its juice and work until smooth. Season with salt and pepper, then pour over the fish.
4. Cover and cook on HIGH for 6 minutes.
5. Stir in the blended cornflour, being careful not to break up the fish, and cook on HIGH for 3 minutes or until the sauce thickens. Serve with boiled rice.

STUFFED COD STEAKS

4 cod cutlets, each about
  2.5 cm (1 inch) thick
25 g (1 oz) butter
1 small onion, chopped
50 g (2 oz) fresh
  breadcrumbs
1 tablespoon chopped
  parsley

pinch of dried mixed herbs
1 tablespoon grated
  Parmesan cheese
2 tablespoons milk
salt and pepper to taste
2 tablespoons lemon juice
lemon wedges sprinkled
  with parsley to garnish

1. Cut away the centre bone from each cod cutlet, then arrange the cutlets in a microwave dish.

2. Place the butter in a bowl and microwave on HIGH for 30 seconds. Add the onion and cook for 2 minutes. Stir in the breadcrumbs, parsley, dried herbs, Parmesan cheese, and salt and pepper, then add the milk to bind the stuffing together.

3. Spoon the stuffing into the eye of the cutlets, sprinkle with lemon juice, cover and cook on HIGH for 6 minutes.

4. Garnish with lemon wedges to serve.

Serves 4
Preparation time: 20 minutes
Power setting: HIGH
Cooking time: 8½ minutes

SPICED RICE CHICKEN

25 g (1 oz) butter
1 tablespoon oil
350 g (12 oz) boneless
   skinned chicken breasts
1 onion, chopped
1 clove garlic, crushed
1 teaspoon each ground
   cumin and coriander
1/2 teaspoon ground
   ginger

1/2 teaspoon turmeric
150 ml (1/4 pint) pure
   orange juice
450 ml (1/4 pint) hot
   chicken stock
250 g (8 oz) long-grain
   rice
50 g (2 oz) sultanas
salt and pepper to taste
coriander leaves to garnish

Serves 4
Preparation time:
10 minutes
Power setting:
HIGH
Cooking time:
21 minutes
Standing time:
5 minutes

1. Place the butter and oil in a large bowl and microwave on HIGH for 1 minute. Cut the chicken into small pieces and add to the bowl with the onion and garlic. Cover and cook on HIGH for 5 minutes.
2. Stir in the spices, orange juice, stock and rice, season with salt and pepper, then cover and cook on HIGH for 15 minutes.
3. Add the sultanas, then leave to stand for 5 minutes. Garnish with coriander and serve with a cucumber salad.

CHICKEN LIVERS WITH SAGE

50 g (2 oz) butter
1 onion, sliced
1 clove garlic, crushed
25 g (1 oz) plain flour
500 g (1 lb) chicken livers
250 g (8 oz) button
   mushrooms, sliced

1 tablespoon dry white
   wine
142 ml (5 fl oz) carton
   soured cream
1 tablespoon chopped sage
salt and pepper to taste
sage leaves to garnish

Serves 4
Preparation time:
10 minutes
Power setting:
HIGH
Cooking time:
12 minutes

1. Place the butter in a large shallow dish and microwave on HIGH for 1 minute. Add the onion and garlic, cover and cook for 3 minutes.
2. Season the flour with salt and pepper and use to coat the chicken livers. Add to the dish, stir and cook on HIGH for 2 minutes.
3. Add the mushrooms, cover and cook on HIGH for 3 minutes. Stir in the wine and soured cream, add the sage, and salt and pepper and stir gently to mix. Cook on HIGH for 3 minutes.
4. Garnish with sage leaves and serve immediately, with creamed potatoes or pasta and a green vegetable.

BOBOTIE

25 g (1 oz) butter	25 g (1 oz) fresh
1 tablespoon oil	breadcrumbs
2 onions, chopped	2 eggs
1 clove garlic, crushed	150 ml (¼ pint) milk
3 teaspoons curry powder	25 g (1 oz) flaked
750 g (1½ lb) minced beef	almonds, toasted
50 g (2 oz) sultanas	3 bay leaves
1 tablespoon chutney	salt and pepper to taste

Serves 4
Preparation time:
10 minutes
Power setting:
HIGH
Cooking time:
25 minutes
Standing time:
5 minutes

1. Place the butter and oil in a large bowl and microwave on HIGH for 1 minute. Add the onions and garlic, cover and cook for 2 minutes. Stir in the curry powder and cook on HIGH for 2 minutes.
2. Mix in the minced beef and cook on HIGH for 5 minutes. Add the sultanas, chutney, breadcrumbs, 1 egg, and salt and pepper and mix well. Turn into a microwave serving dish.
3. Beat the remaining egg and milk together, pour over the meat, then sprinkle with the almonds. Place the bay leaves on top, then cook on HIGH for 15 minutes. Leave to stand, covered, for 5 minutes.

LEMON CHICKEN

1 tablespoon oil	1 teaspoon grated fresh
500 g (1 lb) boneless	root ginger
skinned chicken breasts,	shredded rind of 1 lemon
cut into thin strips	5 spring onions, chopped
4 small courgettes, sliced	2 tablespoons dry sherry
thinly	2 tablespoons soy sauce
2 carrots, sliced thinly	juice of ½ lemon
	2 teaspoons cornflour

Serves 4
Preparation time:
15 minutes
Power setting:
HIGH
Cooking time:
12 minutes

1. Place the oil in a bowl and microwave on HIGH for 1 minute, add the chicken and cook on HIGH for 2 minutes.
2. Add the courgettes, carrots and ginger and cook on HIGH for 3 minutes.
3. Stir in the lemon rind, spring onions, sherry and soy sauce, cover and cook on HIGH for 3 minutes.
4. Blend the lemon juice and cornflour together, stir into the dish, cover and cook on HIGH for 3 minutes, until the sauce thickens.
5. Serve with boiled rice and prawn crackers.

MEXICAN MEATBALLS

50 g (2 oz) bread, crusts
    removed
500 g (1 lb) minced beef
1 small onion, chopped
    finely
1 clove garlic, crushed
1 tablespoon chopped
    parsley
1/2 teaspoon chilli powder,
    or to taste
1/2 teaspoon ground
    cumin
FOR THE SAUCE:
1 tablespoon oil
1 small onion, chopped
    finely

1 green pepper, cored,
    seeded and chopped
1 tablespoon plain flour
300 ml (1/2 pint) tomato
    juice
1 tablespoon tomato purée
1 beef stock cube, blended
    with 4 tablespoons
    boiling water
1 teaspoon chilli sauce
1 teaspoon chopped
    oregano
432 g (15 1/4 oz) can red
    kidney beans, drained
salt and pepper to taste

Serves 4
Preparation time:
20 minutes
Power setting:
HIGH
Cooking time:
14 minutes

1. Soak the bread in water to cover for 5 minutes, then squeeze dry and mash. Add the remaining ingredients, with salt and pepper, and mix well.
2. Divide the mixture into 16 balls. Arrange in a single layer in a shallow dish and cook on HIGH for 5 minutes.
3. To make the sauce, put the oil and onion in a large shallow dish, cover and cook on HIGH for 2 minutes. Add the green pepper and cook for 1 minute.
4. Stir in the flour, then blend in the tomato juice and tomato purée. Add the remaining ingredients, with salt and pepper. Cover and cook on HIGH for 3 minutes.
5. Add the meatballs and their juices to the sauce and cook on HIGH for 3 minutes.
6. Serve with boiled rice and green salad.

BEEF AND OLIVE CASSEROLE

2 tablespoons olive oil
1 large onion, sliced
1 clove garlic, crushed
750 g (1 1/2 lb) braising
    steak, cut into 5 cm
    (2 inch) cubes
300 ml (1/2 pint) red wine
1 beef stock cube
150 ml (1/4 pint) boiling
    water

2 long strips pared orange
    zest
1 bouquet garni
125 g (4 oz) pitted black
    olives
125 g (4 oz) button
    mushrooms, quartered
25 g (1 oz) butter
1 tablespoon plain flour
salt and pepper to taste

1. Place the oil, onion and garlic in a bowl and cook on HIGH for 3 minutes.
2. Add the braising steak, wine, crumbled stock cube, water, orange zest and bouquet garni and stir well. Cover and cook on HIGH for 10 minutes. Stir again, then cover and cook on LOW for 20 minutes.
3. Stir in the olives and mushrooms, cover and cook on LOW for 20 minutes. Remove the orange zest and bouquet garni.
4. Blend the butter and flour together to make a *beurre manié* paste, then stir into the casserole. Cover and cook on LOW for 10 minutes.
5. Leave to stand for 5–10 minutes. Serve with boiled rice.

Serves 4
Preparation time:
15 minutes
Power setting:
HIGH and LOW
Cooking time:
1 hour 3 minutes
Standing time:
5–10 minutes

SAUSAGE COBBLER

Children will love the scone topping on this dish. The leeks could be changed to any vegetable of your choice, such as cauliflower, carrots or a can of borlotti or white kidney beans.

*500 g (1 lb) thick pork
    sausages
1 tablespoon oil
500 g (1 lb) leeks, sliced
40 g (1½ oz) butter
40 g (1½ oz) plain flour
450 ml (¾ pint) milk
1 teaspoon chopped mixed
    herbs
salt and pepper to taste*

*FOR THE SCONE
    TOPPING:
250 g (8 oz) wholemeal
    self-raising flour
1 teaspoon baking powder
1 teaspoon dry mustard
50 g (2 oz) margarine
50 g (2 oz) Cheddar
    cheese, grated
1 egg
3–4 tablespoons milk*

**Serves 4
Preparation time:**
25 minutes
Power setting:
HIGH
Cooking time:
21 minutes

1. Prick the sausages, place in a large shallow dish with the oil and cook on HIGH for 4 minutes, turning once. Drain on kitchen paper, discarding the oil and any fat. Leave to cool, then cut each sausage into 3 pieces.
2. Place the leeks in the dish with 3 tablespoons water, cover and cook on HIGH for 5 minutes. Drain and set aside.
3. Place the butter in a bowl and microwave on HIGH for 1 minute. Stir in the flour, then gradually blend in the milk. Cook on HIGH for 4 minutes, stirring twice. Add the herbs, and salt and pepper.
4. Add the leeks and sausages to the white sauce, then spoon into a round dish.
5. To make the scone topping, mix together the flour, baking powder, mustard and a pinch of salt. Rub in the margarine, then stir in the cheese.
6. Beat the egg and milk together. Set aside 1 tablespoon, then mix the rest into the rubbed-in mixture to make a soft dough.
7. Roll out the dough on a floured surface to a 1 cm (½ inch) thickness, then cut into rounds using a 5 cm (2 inch) plain cutter.
8. Lay the scones, slightly overlapping, on top of the sausage mixture, around the edge of the dish. Brush the scones with the reserved egg and milk mixture. Cook on HIGH for 7 minutes. Serve immediately.

ORANGE PORK CHOPS

4 pork chops
microwave browning
    agent
25 g (1 oz) butter
juice of 1 orange
1 tablespoon orange
    marmalade

2 rosemary sprigs, divided
    into pieces
1 teaspoon cornflour,
    blended with
    1 tablespoon water
salt and pepper to taste
orange wedges to garnish

1. Sprinkle the chops with salt, pepper and microwave browning agent. Preheat a microwave browning skillet for 8 minutes, then allow the butter to melt on it. Place the chops on the hot skillet and cook on HIGH for 3 minutes. Turn the chops and cook on HIGH for 2 minutes.
2. Add the orange juice, marmalade and rosemary. Cover and cook on HIGH for 4 minutes.
3. Transfer the chops to a warmed serving dish, cover with foil and leave to stand for 2 minutes.
4. Meanwhile, add the orange juices from the skillet to the blended cornflour, then cook on HIGH for 2 minutes.
5. Pour over the chops and garnish with orange to serve.

Serves 4
Preparation time:
20 minutes
Power setting:
HIGH
Cooking time:
11 minutes
Standing time:
2 minutes

MEDITERRANEAN LAMB

A succulent way of cooking a shoulder of lamb. Boning
makes carving so much easier and the stuffing adds extra
flavours to the meat. Serve for a special family meal.

1 tablespoon olive oil
1 small onion, chopped
  finely
1 clove garlic, crushed
50 g (2 oz) button
  mushrooms, chopped
  finely
75 g (3 oz) risotto rice,
  cooked
12 stuffed olives, chopped
  finely
1 teaspoon chopped
  oregano
1 tablespoon chopped
  parsley

1 shoulder of lamb,
  weighing 1½–2 kg
  (3½–4½ lb), boned
150 ml (¼ pint) dry white
  wine
1 teaspoon paprika
2 tablespoons tomato
  purée
1 each green, red and
  yellow pepper, cored
  and seeded
1 tablespoon cornflour,
  blended with
  2 tablespoons water
salt and pepper to taste

Serves 6–8
Preparation time:
30 minutes, plus
cooking rice
Power setting:
HIGH and
MEDIUM
Cooking time:
48 minutes–
1 hour,
approximately
Standing time:
25 minutes

1. Place the oil, onion and garlic in a small bowl, cover and
cook on HIGH for 2 minutes. Add the mushrooms and
cook for 1 minute. Stir in the rice, olives, herbs, and salt
and pepper.
2. Place the lamb skin side down on a board and season
well. Spread the rice mixture over the meat, roll up and tie
securely with string. Weigh the joint and calculate the
cooking time, allowing 12 minutes per 500 g (1 lb) on
MEDIUM.
3. Place the lamb in a roasting bag in a dish and cook on
MEDIUM for half of the calculated cooking time. Remove
from the bag and place in the dish.
4. Mix the wine, paprika and tomato purée together, then
pour over the lamb.
5. Cut the peppers into strips or chunks, then place
around the lamb. Cover and cook on MEDIUM for the
remaining cooking time.
6. Pour off the juices into a jug. Cover the lamb and
peppers and leave to stand for 25 minutes.
7. Skim off the fat from the juices, add the blended
cornflour and cook on HIGH for 3 minutes. Stir in the
peppers and season with salt and pepper if necessary.
8. Serve the lamb carved in slices with the sauce served
separately.

MIDDLE EASTERN LAMB KEBABS

750 g (1½ lb) boneless leg
  of lamb or neck fillet,
  cut into 2.5 cm (1 inch)
  cubes
125 g (4 oz) dried apricots,
  soaked overnight
FOR THE MARINADE:
4 tablespoons olive oil
1 tablespoon wine vinegar

1 teaspoon ground cumin
1 small onion, chopped
  finely
1 clove garlic, chopped
  finely
1 tablespoon finely
  chopped parsley
salt and pepper to taste

1. Combine the marinade ingredients together in a bowl.
Add the lamb, tossing to make sure each piece is covered.
Cover and chill for about 8 hours, stirring occasionally.
2. Thread the lamb and apricots alternately on 4 wooden
or bamboo skewers and arrange on a microwave roasting
rack or large dish. Cover with greaseproof paper and cook
on MEDIUM for 10 minutes.
3. Serve with plain boiled rice and a salad.

Serves 4
Preparation time:
15 minutes, plus
marinating
Power setting:
MEDIUM
Cooking time:
10 minutes

POTATO CAKE

This dish could be made into a substantial snack by adding chopped ham or salami.

250 g (8 oz) potatoes, grated
1 small onion, grated

1 tablespoon chopped parsley
25 g (1 oz) butter
salt and pepper to taste

Serves 2
Preparation time: 18 minutes
Power setting: HIGH
Cooking time: 10 minutes

1. Preheat a browning skillet on HIGH for 8 minutes.
2. Meanwhile, mix together the potato, onion, parsley, and salt and pepper.
3. Place the butter on the hot skillet and microwave on HIGH for 1 minute. Quickly add the potato mixture, patting it down to a round shape with a fork. Cook on HIGH for 4 minutes.
4. Invert the potato cake onto a flat baking sheet, then slide it straight back onto the skillet. Cook for 5 minutes. Serve immediately.

SESAME CARROTS

Sesame seeds not only give the carrots a crunchy texture, but they are also rich in calcium and have a nutty flavour.

500 g (1 lb) carrots, cut into thin slices
1 tablespoon sesame seeds

25 g (1 oz) butter
salt and pepper to taste

Serves 4
Preparation time: 10 minutes
Power setting: HIGH
Cooking time: 12 minutes
Standing time: 2 minutes

1. Place the carrots and 3 tablespoons water in a dish, cover and cook on HIGH for 8 minutes, stirring halfway through cooking. Leave to stand for 2 minutes.
2. Put the sesame seeds in a shallow container and cook on HIGH for 2 minutes. Set aside.
3. Drain the carrots, add the butter and cook on HIGH for 2 minutes. Season with salt and pepper and toss well.
4. Spoon into a warmed serving dish and sprinkle with the sesame seeds to serve.

CARROT AND CHEESE RING

This vegetable dish would make a good accompaniment to a vegetarian meal. It is also quite delicious cold.

*750 g (1½ lb) carrots,
  grated
3 spring onions, chopped
  finely
50 g (2 oz) Red Leicester
  cheese, grated*

*3 tablespoons milk
1 egg, beaten
2 tablespoons chopped
  parsley
salt and pepper to taste
watercress sprigs to garnish*

**Serves 6
Preparation time:**
15 minutes
Power setting:
HIGH
Cooking time:
13 minutes

1. Place the carrots in a bowl, cover and cook on HIGH for 5 minutes.
2. Add the remaining ingredients, then spoon into a greased 1 litre (1¾ pint) ring mould, pressing evenly.
3. Cover with greaseproof paper and cook on HIGH for 8 minutes. Turn onto a plate and garnish with watercress.

STUFFED COURGETTES

Courgettes with a savoury filling make a delicious starter, vegetarian meal or accompaniment to fish or chicken.

*4 courgettes, halved
  lengthways
1 small onion, chopped
2 tomatoes, skinned,
  seeded and chopped
227 g (8 oz) carton
  cottage cheese
1 tablespoon chopped
  parsley*

*50 g (2 oz) medium
  oatmeal
pinch of cayenne pepper
50 g (2 oz) Cheddar
  cheese, grated finely
salt and pepper to taste
flat-leaved parsley to
  garnish*

Serves 4 as a
starter,
Serves 2 as a
main meal
Preparation time:
20 minutes
Power setting:
HIGH
Cooking time:
12 minutes
Standing time:
2 minutes

1. Using a teaspoon, scoop out the centres from the courgette halves. Sprinkle the insides of the courgette shells with salt and pepper and set aside.
2. Chop the courgette flesh and place in a bowl with the onion. Cover and cook on HIGH for 3 minutes.
3. Stir in the tomatoes, cottage cheese, parsley, oatmeal, cayenne pepper and salt and pepper.
4. Wipe off the moisture inside the courgette shells with kitchen paper, then fill with the stuffing mixture. Place in a dish and sprinkle with the grated cheese.
5. Cook on HIGH for 9 minutes. Leave to stand for 2 minutes. Garnish with parsley to serve.

CORIANDER MUSHROOMS

2 tablespoons olive oil
2 cloves garlic, crushed
500 g (1 lb) large button
    mushrooms, sliced
    thickly

1 teaspoon coriander
    seeds, crushed
3 tablespoons Greek
    strained yogurt (cow's)
salt and pepper to taste
chopped parsley to garnish

1. Place the oil and garlic in a large shallow dish and cook on HIGH for 2 minutes. Stir in the mushrooms, making sure they are all coated with the oil, and cook for 3 minutes, stirring them halfway through cooking.
2. Mix in the coriander seeds, yogurt, and salt and pepper and cook on HIGH for 1 minute. Sprinkle with parsley and serve immediately.

Serves 4
Preparation time:
10 minutes
Power setting:
HIGH
Cooking time:
6 minutes

LENTIL CURRY

Serve as an accompaniment to a meat or chicken curry, or
as a main course for a vegetarian meal.

1 onion, chopped
2 tablespoons oil
2 teaspoons hot curry
*   powder*
250 g (8 oz) red lentils

750 ml (1¼ pints) hot
*   vegetable stock*
2 tablespoons mango
*   chutney*
salt and pepper to taste

Serves 4–6
Preparation time:
10 minutes
Power setting:
HIGH
Cooking time:
23 minutes

1. Place the onion and oil in a bowl, cover and cook on
HIGH for 2 minutes. Add the curry powder and cook for 1
minute.
2. Stir in the remaining ingredients, cover and cook on
HIGH for 20 minutes. Check the seasoning, stir well then
transfer to a warmed serving dish.

AUBERGINE LAYER

500 g (1 lb) aubergines,
*   cut into 5 mm (¼ inch)*
*   slices*
1 onion, chopped
2 tablespoons oil
1 clove garlic, crushed
250 g (8 oz) mushrooms,
*   chopped*
350 g (12 oz) tomatoes,
*   skinned and chopped*

2 teaspoons tomato purée
1 teaspoon dried oregano
75 g (3 oz) easy-cook
*   lasagne*
150 g (5.3 oz) carton
*   natural yogurt*
1 egg, beaten
2 teaspoons grated
*   Parmesan cheese*
salt and pepper to taste

Serves 4–6
Preparation time:
25 minutes, plus
standing time
Power setting:
HIGH
Cooking time:
32 minutes
Standing time:
5 minutes

1. Sprinkle the aubergine slices with salt, place in a
colander and leave to stand for 1 hour. Rinse well, pat dry
on kitchen paper, then place in a bowl, cover and cook on
HIGH for 4 minutes. Set aside.
2. Place the onion and oil in another bowl and cook on
HIGH for 3 minutes. Add the garlic, mushrooms,
tomatoes, tomato purée, oregano, and salt and pepper,
cover and cook on HIGH for 5 minutes.
3. Arrange a third of the lasagne in a shallow dish, cover
with a third of the tomato sauce, and finish with a third of
the aubergine slices. Repeat these layers twice.
4. Beat the yogurt and egg together, season with salt and
pepper, then spoon over the aubergines. Sprinkle with the
Parmesan and cook on HIGH for 20 minutes.
5. Leave to stand for 5 minutes. Serve with salad.

TOMATO AND POTATO BAKE

350 g (12 oz) potatoes,
   sliced thinly
1 large onion, sliced
40 g (1½ oz) butter

500 g (1 lb) tomatoes,
   skinned and sliced
4 tablespoons single cream
½ teaspoon chopped basil
salt and pepper to taste

Serves 4–6
Preparation time:
15 minutes
Power setting:
HIGH
Cooking time:
16 minutes

1. Place the potatoes in a large shallow dish with 4 tablespoons water. Place another fitting dish on top and put into it the onion and butter. Place the 2 dishes in the oven and cook on HIGH for 6 minutes, stirring the onion twice during cooking.
2. Arrange half of the potatoes in a serving dish. Cover with half of the tomatoes, then two thirds of the onion. Spoon over half of the cream and basil, then season with salt and pepper.
3. Repeat the potato and tomato layers, pile the remaining onion in the centre and spoon the remaining cream over the tomatoes. Season with the remaining basil, and salt and pepper, then cook on HIGH for 10 minutes.
4. Serve with any roast meat.

STUFFED PEPPERS

These stuffed peppers make an ideal vegetarian meal.
Serve with a leafy salad and granary bread.

4 large peppers
2 tablespoons oil
1 onion, chopped
3 celery sticks, chopped
125 g (4 oz) mushrooms,
   chopped
125 g (4 oz) wholemeal
   breadcrumbs

50 g (2 oz) Brazil nuts,
   chopped
½ teaspoon dried mixed
   herbs
125 g (4 oz) Cheddar
   cheese, grated
salt and pepper to taste

Serves 4
Preparation time:
15 minutes
Power setting:
HIGH
Cooking time:
15 minutes
Standing time:
2 minutes

1. Slice the tops off the peppers and remove the seeds.
2. Place the oil in a bowl with the onion, cover and cook on HIGH for 3 minutes. Add the celery and mushrooms and cook for 2 minutes.
3. Mix in the remaining ingredients, then spoon into the peppers. Replace the tops and stand the peppers upright close together in a dish.
4. Pour in 3 tablespoons water, cover and cook on HIGH for 10 minutes. Stand for 2 minutes before serving.

SUPPERS & SNACKS

PRAIRIE POTATOES

*4 potatoes, each weighing
250 g (8 oz)
25 g (1 oz) butter
3 tablespoons milk
250 g (8 oz) corned beef,
diced*

*198 g (7 oz) can sweetcorn
kernels, drained
2 tablespoons chutney
125 g (4 oz) Cheddar
cheese, grated
salt and pepper to taste*

Serves 4
Preparation time:
10 minutes
Power setting:
HIGH
Cooking time:
21 minutes
Standing time:
5 minutes

1. Prick the potato skins, wrap each one in kitchen paper and cook on HIGH for 10 minutes. Turn the potatoes over and cook for 7 minutes. Leave to stand for 5 minutes.
2. Cut the potatoes in half and scoop out the flesh into a bowl. Add the butter and milk and mash well. Stir in the corned beef, sweetcorn, chutney, half of the cheese, and salt and pepper.
3. Spoon the filling into the potato skins and top with the remaining cheese. Cook on HIGH for 4 minutes. Serve immediately, with a green salad.

DEVILLED KIDNEY AND MUSHROOMS

*12 lambs' kidneys
25 g (1 oz) butter
1 small onion, chopped
finely
250 g (8 oz) button
mushrooms, quartered
2 teaspoons Dijon mustard*

*1 tablespoon each
Worcestershire sauce and
mushroom ketchup
2 teaspoons cornflour
2 tablespoons single cream
salt and pepper to taste
toast triangles to serve*

Serves 4
Preparation time:
15 minutes
Power setting:
HIGH
Cooking time:
14 minutes

1. Cut the kidneys in half lengthways, remove the membranes and cores and set aside.
2. Place the butter in a shallow dish and microwave on HIGH for 1 minute. Add the onion; cook for 3 minutes.
3. Stir in the kidneys, cover and cook on HIGH for 2 minutes. Add the mushrooms and cook for 3 minutes.
4. Mix the mustard, Worcestershire sauce and mushroom ketchup into the kidneys, stir, cover and cook on HIGH for 3 minutes.
5. Blend the cornflour with the cream, stir into the kidney mixture, cover and cook on HIGH for 2 minutes. Season with salt and pepper. Serve with toast triangles.

PILCHARD PIZZA

1 tablespoon oil
1 small onion, chopped
397 g (14 oz) can chopped
   tomatoes
425 g (15 oz) can
   pilchards in tomato
   sauce, drained
pinch of dried mixed herbs
50 g (2 oz) Cheddar
   cheese, grated

salt and pepper to taste
FOR THE BASE:
250 g (8 oz) self-raising
   flour
1 teaspoon baking powder
pinch of salt
50 g (2 oz) margarine
1 egg, beaten
3 tablespoons milk

Serves 4
Preparation time:
15 minutes
Power setting:
HIGH
Cooking time:
9 minutes

1. Place the oil and onion in a small bowl and cook on HIGH for 2 minutes. Stir in the tomatoes, then set aside.
2. Make the pizza base: sift the flour, baking powder and salt into a bowl, then rub in the margarine until the mixture resembles breadcrumbs. Add the egg and milk and mix to a soft dough.
3. Knead lightly, then roll out on a floured surface to a 25 cm (10 inch) circle. Place on greaseproof paper, set on the microwave turntable or on a large flat plate and cook on HIGH for 4 minutes. Remove the greaseproof and return the scone base to the turntable or plate.
4. Spread the tomatoes over the scone base. Split the pilchards in half and remove the bones, then arrange on top of the tomatoes. Sprinkle with the herbs, salt and pepper, then the grated cheese. Cook the pizza on HIGH for 3 minutes.
5. Serve immediately, with a mixed green salad.

VARIATION
Replace the pilchards with sardines or flaked tuna fish. Add a few anchovies, if liked, arranged in a lattice pattern over the top of the cheese.

FISHERMAN'S PIE

750 g (1½ lb) potatoes,
   sliced thinly
250 g (8 oz) frozen mixed
   vegetables
2 × 198 g (7 oz) cans tuna
   in brine, drained
55 g (1¾ oz) packet onion
   sauce mix

300 ml (½ pint) milk
2 hard-boiled eggs,
   chopped
25 g (1 oz) butter
1 tablespoon finely
   chopped parsley
salt and pepper to taste

1. Place the potatoes in a dish with 6 tablespoons water. Cover and cook on HIGH for 9 minutes. Leave to stand for 5 minutes, then drain.

2. Meanwhile, place the mixed vegetables in a bowl, add 3 tablespoons water, cover and cook on HIGH for 5 minutes. Drain, then return to the bowl.

3. Add the tuna to the vegetables and stir together to break up the tuna chunks a little.

4. Place the onion sauce mix in a jug, stir in the milk, then cook on HIGH for 4 minutes, stirring twice during cooking.

5. Pour the sauce over the tuna and vegetables, add the chopped eggs, and salt and pepper, then spoon into a dish.

6. Add the butter to the potatoes and mash well. Season with salt and pepper, add the parsley and beat thoroughly.

7. Put the potato mixture into a piping bag fitted with a large nozzle and pipe a border around the edge of the dish. Alternatively, spread the potato over the top and mark the surface with a fork. Cook on HIGH for 5 minutes.

Serves 4
Preparation time:
20 minutes
Power setting:
HIGH
Cooking time:
23 minutes
Standing time:
5 minutes

BROCCOLI AND HAM IN CHEESE SAUCE

8 broccoli spears
25 g (1 oz) butter
25 g (1 oz) plain flour
450 ml (¾ pint) milk
1 teaspoon made English
*   mustard*

¼ teaspoon cayenne
*   pepper*
125 g (4 oz) Cheddar
*   cheese, grated*
8 thin slices ham
salt to taste

Serves 4
Preparation time:
10 minutes
Power setting:
HIGH
Cooking time:
16 minutes

1. Arrange the broccoli in a large shallow dish, with the heads in the centre and the stalks radiating out to the sides. Add 4 tablespoons boiling water, cover and cook on HIGH for 8 minutes. Drain and set aside.
2. Place the butter in a bowl and microwave on HIGH for 1 minute. Stir in the flour and microwave for 30 seconds. Gradually stir in the milk, then cook on HIGH for 4 minutes, stirring twice during cooking.
3. Whisk the mustard and cayenne pepper into the sauce, add the cheese and season with salt.
4. Wrap each broccoli spear in a slice of ham, arrange in a dish, then pour over the cheese sauce. Cook on HIGH for 3 minutes. Brown under a hot grill if you wish.
5. Serve immediately, with crusty bread and tomato salad.

MACARONI CHEESE WITH BACON

175 g (6 oz) macaroni
175 g (6 oz) streaky bacon,
*   derinded and chopped*
25 g (1 oz) butter
3 tablespoons plain flour
600 ml (1 pint) milk

1 teaspoon made English
*   mustard*
125 g (4 oz) Cheddar
*   cheese, grated*
salt and pepper to taste

Serves 4
Preparation time:
15 minutes
Power setting:
HIGH
Cooking time:
25 minutes

1. Place the macaroni in a large bowl with 1.2 litres (2 pints) boiling water and a pinch of salt. Cover and cook on HIGH for 10 minutes; drain and keep warm.
2. Place the bacon and butter in a bowl, cover and cook on HIGH for 5 minutes. Stir in the flour, then gradually add the milk. Cook on HIGH, uncovered, for 4 minutes, stirring every minute.
3. Stir the mustard and 75 g (3 oz) of the cheese into the sauce and season with salt and pepper. Fold the macaroni into the sauce, then pour into a casserole.
4. Sprinkle over the remaining cheese and cook, uncovered, on HIGH for 6 minutes.
5. Brown under a hot grill if desired.

TAGLIATELLE WITH CHEESE AND NUTS

For those counting calories, substitute a low-fat soft cheese with herbs and garlic and serve with a green salad. For another variation, substitute chopped ham for the walnuts.

250 g (8 oz) dried
  tagliatelle
1 tablespoon oil
2 tablespoons single
  cream

125 g (4 oz) full-fat soft
  cheese with herbs and
  garlic
75 g (3 oz) walnuts,
  chopped
salt and pepper to taste

Serves 4
Preparation time:
5 minutes
Power setting:
HIGH
Cooking time:
7½ minutes
Standing time:
3 minutes

1. Place the tagliatelle in a large bowl or wide shallow dish, add the oil and 1 teaspoon salt, then pour over 1.2 litres (2 pints) boiling water, making sure the noodles are covered. Cover and cook on HIGH for 6 minutes. Leave to stand for 3 minutes.
2. Drain the noodles, then return to the bowl. Stir in the cream, add the cheese in pieces, then the walnuts. Season with salt and pepper and toss together.
3. Cover and cook on HIGH for 1½ minutes, until the cheese melts.
4. Toss again, then divide between 4 individual dishes and serve immediately.

SPICY INDIAN OMELETTE

This is an unusual way of cooking an omelette. The result is much thicker and more solid than an ordinary omelette, therefore longer, slower cooking is required.

25 g (1 oz) butter
2 tablespoons cornflour
150 g (5.3 oz) carton
  natural yogurt
8 eggs
1 small onion, chopped
  finely
1 tablespoon finely
  chopped parsley

½ teaspoon ground
  coriander
¼ teaspoon chilli powder
¼ teaspoon turmeric
½ teaspoon cumin seeds,
  crushed
50 g (2 oz) frozen peas,
  thawed
salt to taste

1. Place the butter in a large shallow dish and microwave on MEDIUM for 1 minute.
2. Blend the cornflour and yogurt together, beat in the eggs, then add the remaining ingredients.
3. Pour the egg mixture into the dish and cook on MEDIUM for 5 minutes, drawing the edges of the omelette into the centre every minute. Cook for a further 5 minutes on MEDIUM.
4. Leave to stand for 1 minute, then cut into wedges and serve with a tomato and cucumber salad and poppadoms.

Serves 4
Preparation time:
10 minutes
Power setting:
MEDIUM
Cooking time:
11 minutes
Standing time:
1 minute

PAELLA

Paella is Spain's most famous dish, the main ingredients being rice, olive oil and saffron. It can be simple, but for a special occasion the addition of shellfish, spicy sausage and meat makes it very colourful and an ideal dish to serve for a buffet.

4 tablespoons olive oil
1 kg (2 lb) chicken, cut into 6 pieces
125 g (4 oz) pork fillet, cut into small cubes
1 onion, chopped finely
2 cloves garlic, chopped finely
1 red pepper, cored, seeded and cut into strips
350 g (12 oz) long-grain rice
½ teaspoon paprika
pinch of powdered saffron (optional)

750 ml (1¼ pints) boiling chicken stock
125 g (4 oz) chorizo or garlic sausage, sliced thinly
6 raw king prawns (optional)
125 g (4 oz) frozen peas, thawed
125 g (4 oz) peeled prawns
227 g (8 oz) can mussels in brine, drained
4 tomatoes, skinned, seeded and chopped
salt and pepper to taste

Serves 6
Preparation time:
30 minutes
Power setting:
HIGH
Cooking time:
32 minutes
Standing time:
12 minutes

1. Pour the oil into a large dish and microwave on HIGH for 2 minutes. Add the chicken pieces, skin side down, cover and cook on HIGH for 5 minutes. Add the pork and cook for 3 minutes. Remove the meats with a slotted spoon and set aside.

2. Add the onion, garlic and red pepper to the bowl and cook on HIGH for 2 minutes. Stir in the rice and mix well, then add the paprika, saffron, if using, and stock. Return the meats to the bowl, cover and cook on HIGH for 15 minutes. Leave to stand for 10 minutes.

3. Stir in the sausage, king prawns, if using, peas, peeled prawns, mussels, tomatoes, and salt and pepper. Cover and cook on HIGH for 5 minutes. Leave to stand for 2 minutes before serving.

CHICKEN KORMA

This mild and creamy curry is traditionally served on special occasions in India. Accompany the dish with rice and poppadoms and hand round dishes of chutney, chopped onion and sliced tomato.

1.5 kg (3–3½ lb) chicken, cut into 8 pieces and skinned
150 g (5.3 oz) carton natural yogurt
2 cloves garlic, crushed
2 teaspoons turmeric
40 g (1½ oz) butter
1 large onion, sliced
5 cm (2 inch) piece fresh root ginger, peeled and cut into thin strips
½ teaspoon chilli powder

1 teaspoon coriander seeds, crushed
5 whole cloves
1 teaspoon salt
5 cm (2 inch) piece cinnamon stick
2 teaspoons cornflour
142 ml (5 fl oz) carton single cream
25 g (1 oz) unsalted cashew nuts, browned (see page 7)

Serves 4
Preparation time: 20 minutes, plus marinating
Power setting: HIGH and MEDIUM
Cooking time: 21 minutes
Standing time: 5 minutes

1. Place the chicken pieces in a dish. Mix together the yogurt, garlic and turmeric and pour over the chicken. Cover and leave to marinate overnight in the refrigerator.
2. Place the butter in a large casserole and microwave on HIGH for 1 minute. Add the onion and cook for 3 minutes.
3. Stir the ginger, chilli powder and coriander into the onion and cook on HIGH for 1 minute.
4. Add the chicken with its marinade, the cloves, salt and cinnamon stick, cover and cook on HIGH for 7 minutes.
5. Stir and rearrange the chicken pieces, then cook on MEDIUM for 6 minutes.
6. Blend the cornflour with the cream, stir into the chicken and cook on HIGH for 3 minutes. Leave to stand for 5 minutes. Sprinkle with the nuts to serve.

POUSSINS CHAMPENOISE

This delicious dinner party dish is made with inexpensive sparkling wine and garnished with grapes.

4 poussins
75 g (3 oz) butter
300 ml (½ pint) dry sparkling white wine
1 chicken stock cube

250 g (8 oz) seedless grapes
2 tablespoons plain flour
salt and pepper to taste

1. Season the poussins inside and out with salt and pepper and put a knob of butter inside each body cavity.
2. Heat a browning skillet on HIGH for 8 minutes. Add 25 g (1 oz) of the remaining butter to the skillet and microwave on HIGH for 1 minute.
3. Place the poussins, breasts down, on the skillet and cook on HIGH for 2 minutes. Turn the birds over and cook for 2 minutes.
4. Transfer the poussins to a large casserole, pour over the wine and add the stock cube. Cover and cook on HIGH for 15 minutes.
5. Add the grapes and cook on HIGH for 5 minutes.
6. Remove the poussins with a slotted spoon and discard any trussing string. Place on a warmed serving dish.
7. Remove the grapes with a slotted spoon and arrange around the poussins. Cover with foil to keep warm.
8. Blend the remaining butter with the flour, whisk into the cooking liquid and cook on HIGH for 6 minutes, stirring twice, until thickened. Season with salt and pepper.
9. Pour a little sauce over the poussins and serve the remaining sauce separately.

Serves 4
Preparation time: 30 minutes
Power setting: HIGH
Cooking time: 31 minutes

TARRAGON TROUT

50 g (2 oz) butter
1 small onion, chopped
250 g (8 oz) button
   mushrooms, chopped
1 tablespoon chopped
   tarragon
4 trout, cleaned

2 tablespoons dry white
   wine
salt and pepper to taste
TO GARNISH:
lemon slices
tarragon sprigs

Serves 4
Preparation time:
10 minutes
Power setting:
HIGH
Cooking time:
16 minutes

1. Place the butter in a bowl and microwave on HIGH for 1 minute. Add the onion and cook on HIGH for 1 minute. Stir in the mushrooms and cook for 2 minutes. Add the tarragon, and salt and pepper.
2. Make 2 slits on each side of each fish to prevent the skin from bursting during cooking. Divide the mushroom mixture between the trout, stuffing it into the body cavity. Shield the tails with foil.
3. Place the fish in a shallow dish, pour over the wine, cover and cook on HIGH for 12 minutes, changing the position of the fish halfway through cooking.
4. Garnish with the lemon slices and tarragon to serve.

SALMON WITH DILL SAUCE

4 salmon steaks, about
   2.5 cm (1 inch) thick
4 tablespoons water
juice of ½ lemon
2 egg yolks

125 g (4 oz) butter
1 tablespoon chopped dill
salt and pepper to taste
dill sprigs to garnish

Serves 4
Preparation time:
10 minutes
Power setting:
HIGH
Cooking time:
8 minutes

1. Arrange the salmon in a large shallow dish. Mix the water with 1 tablespoon of the lemon juice, season with salt, then pour over the fish.
2. Cover with greaseproof paper and cook on HIGH for 6 minutes. Set aside while making the sauce.
3. Place the egg yolks in a blender or food processor and blend for 30 seconds. Place the butter in a dish and microwave on HIGH for 1 minute, then add the remaining lemon juice.
4. With the motor running, pour the butter in a steady stream onto the egg yolks until combined. Pour into a bowl and stir in the chopped dill and salt and pepper.
5. Arrange the salmon on a warmed serving plate and spoon a little of the sauce over each portion. Garnish each with a sprig of dill.

SEAFOOD AND WATERCRESS SOUFFLÉ

This unusual dish has a layer of creamy fish and a layer of watercress soufflé—light in texture and rich in flavour. Use any combination of white fish: try monkfish and lemon sole for a special occasion and a few sliced scallops for extra luxury.

500 g (1 lb) white fish, e.g. plaice fillets, lemon sole, skinned
2 tablespoons dry white wine
2 teaspoons cornflour
3 tablespoons double cream
6 eggs, separated
125 g (4 oz) peeled prawns
40 g (1½ oz) butter
40 g (1½ oz) plain flour

300 ml (½ pint) milk
¼ teaspoon ground mace
pinch of cayenne pepper
2 bunches watercress, chopped finely
2 tablespoons grated Parmesan cheese
salt and pepper to taste
TO GARNISH:
watercress sprigs
unpeeled prawns

Serves 4
Preparation time:
25 minutes
Power setting:
HIGH
Cooking time:
18 minutes
Standing time:
2 minutes

1. Cut the fish into 2.5 cm (1 inch) pieces and place in a dish. Sprinkle with the wine, cover and cook on HIGH for 3 minutes. Drain thoroughly, reserving the liquor.
2. Blend together the cornflour, cream and 1 egg yolk in a bowl, then gradually stir in the fish liquor. Cook on HIGH for 2 minutes, whisking every 30 seconds. Whisk again until smooth and season with salt and pepper.
3. Carefully fold the cooked fish and the prawns into the sauce, then spoon into a greased 23 cm (9 inch) soufflé dish or microwave container.
4. Place the butter in a large bowl and microwave on HIGH for 1 minute. Beat in the flour, then gradually add the milk. Cook on HIGH for 2 minutes, stirring every 30 seconds, then give the sauce a good whisk until glossy. Season with the mace, cayenne, and salt and pepper.
5. Add the remaining egg yolks, beating well after each addition, then stir in the watercress and Parmesan cheese.
6. Whisk the egg whites until stiff, then carefully fold into the watercress mixture. Pour into the dish, covering the fish evenly, and cook on HIGH for 10 minutes.
7. Leave to stand for 2 minutes; the soufflé will shrink away from the edge.
8. Carefully turn out onto a warmed serving plate and garnish with watercress and prawns to serve.

VEAL CHOPS WITH RED PEPPER SAUCE

4 veal chops
microwave seasoning
1 small onion, chopped
2 red peppers, cored,
    seeded and chopped

1 clove garlic, chopped
150 ml (¼ pint) light stock
2 tablespoons oil
salt and pepper to taste
snipped chives to garnish

1. Sprinkle the chops with the microwave seasoning and set aside.
2. Place the onion in a bowl, cover and cook on HIGH for 2 minutes. Add the red pepper, garlic and stock, cover and cook on HIGH for 10 minutes. Leave to stand for 10 minutes.
3. Meanwhile, heat a browning skillet on HIGH for 8 minutes. Pour over the oil and heat for 2 minutes.
4. Place the veal chops on the skillet and cook on HIGH for 6 minutes on each side.
5. While they are cooking, place the red pepper mixture in a blender or food processor and work until smooth. Season with salt and pepper if necessary. Reheat the sauce on HIGH for 2 minutes just before serving.
6. Pour the red pepper sauce over the chops and garnish with chives. Serve with mangetouts.

Serves 4
Preparation time:
30 minutes
Power setting:
HIGH
Cooking time:
24 minutes

SWEET AND SOUR PORK

*227 g (8 oz) can pineapple
  slices in natural juice
2 tablespoons soy sauce
3 tablespoons pure orange
  juice
1 tablespoon lemon juice
2 tablespoons tomato
  ketchup
2 tablespoons olive oil*

*1 tablespoon clear honey
1 tablespoon grated fresh
  root ginger
1 kg (2 lb) pork tenderloin,
  cut into 5 mm (¼ inch)
  slices
2 tablespoons cornflour
salt and pepper to taste*

**Serves 4–6
Preparation time:**
10 minutes, plus
marinating
Power setting:
HIGH
Cooking time:
12 minutes

1. Drain the pineapple, reserving the juice, and cut the slices into quarters. Set aside.
2. Place the soy sauce, orange and lemon juice, ketchup, oil, honey and ginger in a large bowl. Add half of the pineapple juice and mix well. Add the pork, toss well to coat in the marinade, cover and chill for 2 hours.
3. Cover the bowl and cook on HIGH for 5 minutes. Add the pineapple.
4. Blend the cornflour with the remaining pineapple juice, stir into the pork, and season with salt and pepper. Cover and cook on HIGH for 7 minutes.
5. Serve with boiled rice or egg noodles.

PORK SATÉ

This Indonesian dish consists of marinated cubes of meat cooked on skewers and served with a spicy peanut sauce. For chicken saté, use 500 g (1 lb) boneless chicken breast; for beef saté use 500 g (1 lb) rump steak.

*625 g (1¼ lb) pork
  tenderloin, cut into
  2.5 cm (1 inch) cubes
½ teaspoon chilli powder
½ teaspoon turmeric
1 teaspoon ground
  coriander
1 teaspoon ground cumin
½ teaspoon salt
2 tablespoons soy sauce
1 tablespoon oil*

*FOR THE SAUCE:
1 tablespoon oil
1 very small onion,
  chopped finely
1 clove garlic, crushed
3 tablespoons peanut
  butter
½ teaspoon chilli powder
1 teaspoon light brown soft
  sugar
1 teaspoon lemon juice
TO GARNISH:
spring onion tassels (see
  page 16)*

1. Place the pork in a bowl. Mix together the spices, salt and soy sauce, then mix into the pork, using your hands to knead the spices into the meat. Cover and leave in a cool place to marinate for at least 6 hours.

2. Thread the pork cubes onto bamboo or wooden skewers, brush with the oil and place on a microwave roasting rack or large microwave dish, over a bowl. Cover with greaseproof paper and microwave on MEDIUM for 10 minutes, rearranging and turning the kebabs after 5 minutes. Wrap in foil and leave to stand for 5 minutes.

3. To make the sauce, mix the ingredients together in a bowl and cook on HIGH for 1 minute. Serve hot with the pork. Garnish the dish with spring onion tassels.

Serves 4
Preparation time:
10 minutes, plus marinating
Power setting:
HIGH and MEDIUM
Cooking time:
11 minutes
Standing time:
5 minutes

GAMMON WITH GREEN PEPPER SAUCE

Green peppercorns are pungent in flavour and add spiciness to a dish. They are available fresh, but you may wish to buy some preserved in brine for future use.

*1–1.5 kg (2–3 lb) smoked
    gammon joint, soaked
    overnight
25 g (1 oz) butter
25 g (1 oz) plain flour*

*142 ml (5 fl oz) carton
    single cream
1 tablespoon green
    peppercorns*

Serves 4–6
Preparation time:
10 minutes, plus
overnight soaking
Power setting:
HIGH and
MEDIUM
Cooking time:
27–39 minutes
Standing time:
20 minutes

1. Drain the gammon joint and place in a roasting bag. Tie loosely with string and cook on MEDIUM, allowing 12 minutes per 500 g (1 lb); turn the joint over halfway through cooking.
2. Snip a corner from the roasting bag and pour off the juices into a measuring jug. Skim off any fat from the surface and make up to 150 ml (¼ pint) with water. Leave the joint to stand for 20 minutes.
3. Meanwhile, place the butter in a bowl and microwave on HIGH for 1 minute. Stir in the flour, then the gammon juices and cream. Cook on HIGH for 2 minutes, stirring every 30 seconds. Add the peppercorns and keep warm.
4. Remove the rind from the joint and carve the meat into slices. Arrange on a warmed serving plate, pour over a little sauce and serve the remaining sauce separately.

LAMB IN RED WINE

Boning and rolling lamb is not too difficult but it is quicker and easier to buy ready-prepared noisettes.

*1 kg (2 lb) best end of neck
    of lamb, or 8 noisettes of
    lamb, each 2.5 cm
    (1 inch) thick
250 ml (8 fl oz) red wine
1 clove garlic, crushed*

*few rosemary sprigs
1 tablespoon tomato purée
15 g (½ oz) butter
15 g (½ oz) plain flour
salt and pepper to taste
parsley sprigs to garnish*

1. To prepare noisettes yourself, skin the best end of neck, then place fat side down on a board and cut the meat from the bones with a sharp knife. Season with salt and pepper, roll up tightly and tie at 2.5 cm (1 inch) intervals with fine string. Cut through the meat between the string to make noisettes. Place in a shallow bowl.

2. Mix the wine, garlic, rosemary, tomato purée, and salt and pepper together, then pour over the lamb. Cover and leave to marinate for 3 hours.

3. Cook on HIGH for 8 minutes. Remove lamb, return dish to oven and cook for 5 minutes. Discard the rosemary.

4. Meanwhile, remove string from the lamb and arrange on a warmed serving dish; cover with foil to keep warm.

5. Mash the butter and flour together with a fork, then whisk into the sauce. Cook on HIGH for 2 minutes.

6. Pour over the lamb and garnish with parsley. Serve with new potatoes and a julienne of vegetables.

Serves 4
Preparation time: 25 minutes, plus marinating
Power setting: HIGH
Cooking time: 15 minutes

MOROCCAN FRUIT COMPOTE

500 g (1 lb) dried mixed
    fruits, e.g. apricots,
    apples, pears, prunes or
    figs
150 ml (¼ pint) pure
    orange juice

450 ml (¾ pint) water
2 tablespoons clear honey
1 cinnamon stick
pinch of ground allspice
25 g (1 oz) blanched
    almonds

Serves 6
Preparation time:
5 minutes
Power setting:
HIGH
Cooking time:
15 minutes
Standing time:
Until cool

1. Place the fruits in a large bowl, pour in the orange juice and water, cover and cook on HIGH for 5 minutes.
2. Add the honey, cinnamon stick and allspice, cover and cook on HIGH for 10 minutes.
3. Leave to stand until cool, during which time the fruit will become plumper and more tender. Remove the cinnamon stick, stir in the almonds and chill until required. Serve with crisp biscuits.

CRÈME CARAMELS

125 ml (4 fl oz) water
125 g (4 oz) granulated
    sugar
3 eggs

1 egg yolk
50 g (2 oz) caster sugar
450 ml (¾ pint) milk
1 teaspoon vanilla essence

Serves 6
Preparation time:
10 minutes
Power setting:
HIGH and LOW
Cooking time:
27 minutes

1. Place the water and granulated sugar in a heatproof glass jug and stir well. Cook on HIGH for 11 minutes, until golden; do not allow the syrup to become too brown, as it continues to cook after removal from the oven. Pour quickly into 6 ramekin dishes, then leave to cool and harden.
2. Meanwhile, beat the eggs, egg yolk and caster sugar together.
3. Pour the milk into a jug and cook on HIGH for 4 minutes. Whisk into the egg mixture with the vanilla essence, then strain the mixture back into the jug. Divide between the dishes.
4. Stand the dishes in one container and pour in enough water to come halfway up the sides of the dishes. Cook on LOW for 12 minutes, until set.
5. Remove from the water, leave to cool, then chill.
6. To serve, invert each caramel onto a serving dish.

ORANGE SAVARIN

This impressive-looking cake, soaked in rum-flavoured syrup, is a wonderful dessert for large gatherings.

FOR THE SAVARIN DOUGH:
125 g (4 oz) butter
250 g (8 oz) plain strong white flour
1 sachet easy blend yeast
2 tablespoons caster sugar
1/2 teaspoon salt
5 tablespoons milk, warmed
3 eggs

FOR THE SYRUP:
175 g (6 oz) sugar
300 ml (1/2 pint) water
1 teaspoon lemon juice
6 tablespoons orange juice
6 tablespoons dark rum
TO FINISH:
4 tablespoons marmalade
142 ml (5 fl oz) carton whipping cream, whipped
3 large oranges, peeled and segmented

Serves 12–16
Preparation time:
42 minutes
Power setting:
HIGH
Cooking time:
18 minutes
Standing time:
10 minutes

1. Place the butter in a bowl and microwave on HIGH for 2 minutes.
2. Sift the flour, yeast, 1 tablespoon of the sugar and the salt into a large bowl. Make a well in the centre and pour in the milk.
3. Beat the eggs and remaining sugar until frothy, then add to the flour with the melted butter and beat until smooth. Cover and leave for 10 minutes, then beat the dough with your hand for at least 2 minutes.
4. Spoon the dough into a greased 1.75 litre (3 pint) ring mould and leave to rise in a warm place for about 30–40 minutes, until the mixture reaches the top of the mould.
5. Cook on HIGH for 7 minutes. Leave to stand for 10 minutes, then turn out onto a wire rack. Wash and dry the ring mould, then return the savarin to it.
6. To make the syrup, place the sugar and water in a bowl and microwave on HIGH for 8 minutes, until the sugar has dissolved. Cool until lukewarm, then stir in the fruit juices and rum.
7. Prick the savarin with a skewer and pour over the syrup. Leave to cool, then turn out onto a serving plate.
8. Place the marmalade in a bowl and microwave on HIGH for 1 minute, then brush over the outside of the savarin.
9. Pipe cream around the edge of the savarin and decorate with the orange segments.

TIPSY BREAD PUDDING

*250 g (8 oz) wholemeal
bread, broken into
pieces
125 g (4 oz) raisins
75 g (3 oz) demerara
sugar*

*pinch of mixed spice
4 tablespoons dark rum
450 ml (¾ pint) milk
50 g (2 oz) butter
3 eggs, beaten*

1. Place the bread, raisins, half of the sugar and the mixed spice in a bowl.
2. Mix the rum and milk together, pour over the bread and leave to soak for 30 minutes.
3. Place the butter in a bowl and microwave on HIGH for 2 minutes.
4. Stir the beaten eggs and melted butter into the bread mixture, then pour into 4 or 6 greased ovenproof dishes. Cook on HIGH for 10 minutes.
5. Remove from the oven and sprinkle with the remaining sugar. Leave to stand for 2 minutes. Serve hot or cold with yogurt or whipped cream.

Serves 4–6
Preparation time:
10 minutes, plus
soaking time
Power setting:
HIGH
Cooking time:
12 minutes
Standing time:
2 minutes

CHRISTMAS PUDDING

All the family will love this traditional Christmas pudding, which is not too rich or heavy. Even though it cooks so quickly it can be made in advance and reheated when required.

75 g (3 oz) plain flour
pinch each of salt, nutmeg and cinnamon
1 teaspoon mixed spice
75 g (3 oz) shredded suet
25 g (1 oz) fresh breadcrumbs
75 g (3 oz) dark brown soft sugar
50 g (2 oz) mixed peel
50 g (2 oz) glacé cherries, chopped
50 g (2 oz) currants
125 g (4 oz) sultanas

150 g (5 oz) raisins
50 g (2 oz) cooking apple, peeled and chopped
50 g (2 oz) blanched almonds, chopped
grated rind and juice of ½ lemon
grated rind and juice of 1 small orange
2 tablespoons brandy
2 eggs, beaten
2 tablespoons black treacle
2 tablespoons milk

Serves 6–8
Preparation time:
25 minutes, plus chilling time
Power setting:
HIGH
Cooking time:
10 minutes
Standing time:
10 minutes

1. Sift the flour, salt and spices together into a large bowl. Add the suet, breadcrumbs, sugar, peel, fruit and almonds, then beat in the remaining ingredients to form a soft dropping consistency. Cover and chill overnight.
2. Stir the mixture well, then place in a greased 1.2 litre (2 pint) pudding basin. Cover with greased greaseproof paper or clingfilm and secure with string or elastic band.
3. Cook on HIGH for 10 minutes. Leave to stand for 10 minutes before turning out.
4. To reheat, turn out the pudding onto a serving plate and cover with clingfilm. Cook on HIGH, allowing 1 minute per 500 g (1 lb). Leave to stand for 1 minute.
5. Serve hot, decorated with holly leaves if wished, with whipped cream or brandy butter.

STRAWBERRY GALETTE

150 g (5 oz) unsalted butter
50 g (2 oz) icing sugar, sifted
few drops almond essence
175 g (6 oz) plain flour, sifted

50 g (2 oz) blanched almonds, chopped finely
500 g (1 lb) strawberries, halved
284 ml (10 fl oz) carton double cream, whipped
icing sugar to dust

1. Cream the butter, icing sugar and almond essence together in a bowl, then gradually work in the flour and almonds. Work the mixture until it binds together.

2. Divide the dough in half and press out to a 20 cm (8 inch) round on a piece of non-stick paper placed on the turntable. Prick all over and cook on LOW for 6 minutes. Leave to stand for 2 minutes.

3. Gently place a 20 cm (8 inch) round cake tin on top of the biscuit and, while it is still warm, neaten the edge with a sharp knife.

4. Repeat the cooking procedure with the second half of the dough. After neatening, cut this biscuit into 8 wedges. Leave both biscuits to cool.

5. Place the biscuit round on a flat serving plate and cover with half of the strawberries. Spread with the cream, then top with the remaining strawberries. Arrange the biscuit wedges on top and sprinkle with a little icing sugar.

Serves 6
Preparation time:
25 minutes
Power setting:
LOW
Cooking time:
12 minutes
Standing time:
4 minutes

CONTINENTAL CHEESECAKE

This cake can be decorated with fruit of your choice. Serve thin slices as it is very rich.

50 g (2 oz) butter
50 g (2 oz) caster sugar
3 tablespoons clear honey
2 eggs, beaten
2×227 g (8 oz) cartons
  curd cheese
grated rind and juice of
  ½ lemon
142 ml (5 fl oz) carton
  soured cream
2 teaspoons cornflour

1 teaspoon vanilla essence
50 g (2 oz) sultanas
FOR THE BASE:
50 g (2 oz) butter
1 tablespoon golden syrup
125 g (4 oz) ginger thin
  biscuits, crushed
TO DECORATE:
142 ml (5 fl oz) carton
  double cream, whipped
slices of fruit, e.g. kiwi

Serves 10–12
Preparation time:
25 minutes
Power setting:
HIGH and
DEFROST
Cooking time:
21 minutes

1. Grease the base and sides of a 1.5 litre (2½ pint) microwave loaf dish and line with clingfilm.
2. Beat together the butter, sugar and honey, then gradually add the eggs. Beat in the cheese, lemon rind and juice, soured cream, cornflour and vanilla essence and mix until smooth. Fold in the sultanas.
3. Spoon into the prepared dish, cover with clingfilm and cook on DEFROST for 20 minutes. Remove the cover.
4. Place the butter and syrup in a bowl and microwave on HIGH for 1 minute. Stir in the biscuit crumbs, then spoon on top of the cheesecake, pressing down gently. Leave to cool, then chill until required.
5. Invert the cake onto a serving plate and remove the clingfilm. Decorate with the cream and fruit.

BLACKCURRANT TART

Blackberries, raspberries, strawberries and gooseberries go well with the creamy filling, too.

FOR THE PASTRY:
175 g (6 oz) plain flour
125 g (4 oz) butter, cut
  into small pieces
50 g (2 oz) caster sugar
grated rind and juice of 1
  lemon

FOR THE FILLING:
250 g (8 oz) skimmed milk
  soft cheese
1 egg yolk
142 ml (5 fl oz) carton
  soured cream
500 g (1 lb) blackcurrants
4 tablespoons blackcurrant
  jelly or conserve

1. Sift the flour into a bowl, then rub in the butter until the mixture resembles fine breadcrumbs. Stir in the sugar, add the lemon rind and enough juice to make a firm dough; knead well.

2. Roll out the pastry on a floured board and use to line a greased 23 cm (9 inch) fluted flan dish. Trim the edges and chill for 30 minutes.

3. Prick the base with a fork, then line the base with a double thickness of kitchen paper. Cook on HIGH for 3 minutes. Remove the kitchen paper and cook for 1½ minutes.

4. Beat the cheese, egg yolk and soured cream together, then pour into the flan case. Cook on LOW for 6 minutes or until set. Leave to cool.

5. Meanwhile, place the blackcurrants and jelly or jam in a bowl and cook on HIGH for 3 minutes. Leave to cool, then spoon on top of the flan. Chill until set.

Serves 6–8
Preparation time:
30 minutes, plus chilling time
Power setting:
HIGH and LOW
Cooking time:
13½ minutes

CHOCOLATE FONDUE

Popular with adults and children, this is a scrumptious way to end a meal. Serve any selection of fruit in season to dip into the fondue.

250 g (8 oz) Toblerone
142 ml (5 fl oz) carton
double cream

TO SERVE:
selection of fruit, sliced

Serves 6–8
Preparation time:
15 minutes
Power setting:
MEDIUM
Cooking time:
3 minutes

1. Break the chocolate into pieces and place in a bowl. Add the cream and microwave on MEDIUM for 3 minutes, stirring during cooking, until melted.
2. Pour the fondue into a bowl. Place the bowl on a large plate and arrange the slices of fruit attractively on the plate.

BRAMBLE SYLLABUB

This delicious syllabub can be made using any soft fruit, such as blackcurrants, blackberries or raspberries.

500 g (1 lb) brambles
125 g (4 oz) sugar
2 tablespoons Crème de Cassis liqueur

284 ml (10 fl oz) carton double cream, whipped
1 egg white

1. Place the brambles and sugar in a bowl, cover and cook on HIGH for 5 minutes.
2. Press the fruit through a sieve, discarding the seeds. Stir in the liqueur and leave to cool.
3. Fold in the cream.
4. Whisk the egg white until stiff, then fold into the syllabub. Pour into 6 glasses and chill until required.
5. Serve with dessert biscuits or sponge fingers.

Serves 6
Preparation time:
15 minutes
Power setting:
HIGH
Cooking time:
5 minutes

BOOZY COFFEE RING

A favourite dessert for parties—it's easy to make and is always enjoyed by family and friends.

4 eggs
125 g (4 oz) caster sugar
50 g (2 oz) butter
125 g (4 oz) plain flour
300 ml (1/2 pint) warm strong black coffee
2 tablespoons demerara sugar

4 tablespoons brandy or Tia Maria
TO DECORATE:
284 ml (10 fl oz) carton whipping cream, whipped
25 g (1 oz) flaked almonds, toasted (see page 7)

Serves 10–12
Preparation time: 25 minutes
Power setting: HIGH
Cooking time: 6 minutes
Standing time: 10 minutes

1. Whisk the eggs and caster sugar together until very light and fluffy and about trebled in volume.
2. Place the butter in a bowl and microwave on HIGH for 1 minute.
3. Sift the flour over the egg mixture, then pour in the butter in a slow stream. Fold in carefully with a metal spoon, then pour into a greased 1.75 litre (3 pint) ring mould.
4. Cook on HIGH for 5 minutes. Leave to stand for 10 minutes, then turn out onto a wire rack to cool.
5. Return the cake to the cleaned ring mould and prick with a skewer.
6. Mix the coffee and demerara sugar together, stirring to dissolve the sugar. Stir in the brandy or Tia Maria, pour over the cake and leave to soak.
7. Turn out the cake onto a serving plate and cover with the cream. Sprinkle with the almonds.

APPLE AND RASPBERRY CHARLOTTE

A family favourite, this dessert could be made with blackberries or loganberries instead of raspberries.

750 g (1 1/2 lb) cooking apples, peeled and chopped
50 g (2 oz) granulated sugar, or to taste
350 g (12 oz) raspberries, thawed if frozen
50 g (2 oz) butter

250 g (8 oz) wholemeal breadcrumbs
75 g (3 oz) light brown soft sugar
142 ml (5 fl oz) carton double cream, whipped
25 g (1 oz) walnuts, chopped

1. Place the apples in a bowl with 3 tablespoons water, cover and cook on HIGH for 5 minutes, stirring halfway through cooking.

2. Add the granulated sugar and mash with a fork. Leave to cool, then stir in the raspberries.

3. Place the butter in a large flat dish and microwave on HIGH for 1 minute. Stir in the breadcrumbs and brown sugar, spreading out evenly. Cook on HIGH for 12 minutes, stirring 2 or 3 times during cooking. Leave to cool, when the crumbs will become crisp.

4. Spread one third of the crumbs onto the base of a glass bowl. Cover with half of the fruit. Sprinkle with half of the remaining crumbs, then the remaining fruit. Finish with a layer of crumbs.

5. Pipe the cream around the edge of the charlotte and sprinkle with the nuts. Serve as soon as possible.

Serves 6–8
Preparation time:
15 minutes
Power setting:
HIGH
Cooking time:
18 minutes

DATE FLAPJACKS

250 g (8 oz) dates, stoned and chopped	50 g (2 oz) demerara sugar
3 tablespoons water	125 g (4 oz) porridge oats
75 g (3 oz) margarine	125 g (4 oz) wholemeal
1 tablespoon golden syrup	flour

Makes 8
Preparation time:
15 minutes
Power setting:
HIGH
Cooking time:
10 minutes

1. Place the dates and water in a bowl, cover and cook on HIGH for 3 minutes. Mash the soft dates with a fork, adding a little more water if they are too dry to make a spreading consistency.
2. Place the margarine, syrup and sugar in a bowl and microwave on HIGH for 2 minutes, until the margarine has melted. Mix in the oats and flour.
3. Spread one half of the oat mixture over the base of an 18 cm (7 inch) flan dish, then cover with the dates, spreading evenly. Spoon the remaining oat mixture on top and press down well.
4. Cook on HIGH for 5 minutes. Cut into wedges, while still slightly warm. Leave until cold, then remove the flapjacks from the dish.

BANANA AND CHOCOLATE CHIP CAKE

125 g (4 oz) margarine	250 g (8 oz) self-raising flour
125 g (4 oz) light brown soft sugar	1 teaspoon baking powder
2 eggs, beaten	50 g (2 oz) milk chocolate drops
2 large bananas	

Serves 8–10
Preparation:
15 minutes
Power setting:
HIGH
Cooking time:
7 minutes
Standing time:
3 minutes

1. Place the margarine and sugar in a bowl and beat together until light and creamy. Beat in the eggs one at a time.
2. Mash the bananas and beat into the cake mixture.
3. Sift the flour and baking powder together. Fold into the cake mixture with the chocolate drops.
4. Spoon the mixture into a greased 1.75 litre (3 pint) microwave ring mould and cook on HIGH for 7 minutes.
5. Leave to stand for 3 minutes, then turn out and cool on a wire rack.

MINCEMEAT CAKE

Mincemeat gives this cake a delicious, moist flavour. Split and fill with buttercream if you prefer a richer cake.

250 g (8 oz) plain flour
2 teaspoons baking
   powder
½ teaspoon bicarbonate
   of soda
175 g (6 oz) light brown
   soft sugar
125 g (4 oz) butter
150 g (5.3 oz) carton
   natural yogurt

2 eggs, beaten
grated rind of 1 lemon
175 g (6 oz) mincemeat
TO DECORATE:
125 g (4 oz) icing sugar,
   sifted
3 teaspoons lemon juice
angelica
crystallized lemon slices

Makes one 20 cm (8 inch) cake
Preparation time: 20 minutes
Power setting: HIGH
Cooking time: 10 minutes
Standing time: 5 minutes

1. Sift the flour, baking powder and bicarbonate of soda into a bowl, then stir in the sugar.
2. Place the butter in a bowl and microwave on HIGH for 1 minute. Beat into the flour with the yogurt to make a smooth batter. Gradually beat in the eggs and lemon rind, then add the mincemeat.
3. Turn the mixture into a greased deep 20 cm (8 inch) cake dish and cook on HIGH for 8–9 minutes. Leave to stand for 5 minutes, then turn out onto a wire rack to cool.
4. Beat the icing sugar and lemon juice together to make a thick glacé icing. Spread over the top of the cake and decorate with angelica and lemon slices.

ICED GINGERBREAD

Wholemeal flour gives this cake a nuttier texture. Try adding some sultanas or chopped preserved ginger to the mixture.

175 g (6 oz) margarine
4 tablespoons golden syrup
4 tablespoons black treacle
175 g (6 oz) dark brown
   soft sugar
350 g (12 oz) wholemeal
   flour
1 tablespoon each ground
   ginger and baking
   powder

1 teaspoon bicarbonate of
   soda
1 teaspoon salt
1 egg, beaten
300 ml (½ pint) milk
TO DECORATE:
250 g (8 oz) icing sugar,
   sifted
2 tablespoons water
50 g (2 oz) crystallized
   ginger, chopped

1. Grease and base-line a 22 cm (8½ inch) square dish.
2. Place the margarine, syrup, treacle and sugar in a bowl and microwave on HIGH for 2 minutes, until the margarine has melted.
3. Place the flour in a large bowl, then sift in the ginger, baking powder, bicarbonate of soda and salt. Beat in the egg, milk and melted mixture.
4. Pour into the prepared dish and cook on HIGH for 12 minutes. Leave to stand for 10 minutes, then turn out onto a wire rack to cool.
5. Beat the icing sugar with the water to make a thick glacé icing, then spread over the top of the cake. Sprinkle with the chopped ginger. Leave to set, then cut into fingers.

Makes one 25 cm (10 inch) cake
Preparation time: 15 minutes
Power setting: HIGH
Cooking time: 14 minutes
Standing time: 10 minutes

CHOCOLATE COCONUT BROWNIES

These are so quick you can make them within minutes of children arriving home with unexpected friends for tea.

*150 g (5 oz) wholemeal
    self-raising flour
½ teaspoon bicarbonate
    of soda
175 g (6 oz) light brown
    soft sugar
125 g (4 oz) desiccated
    coconut*

*4 tablespoons cocoa
    powder
125 g (4 oz) margarine,
    diced
2 eggs, beaten
150 ml (¼ pint) milk*

Makes 16
Preparation time:
10 minutes
Power setting:
HIGH
Cooking time:
9 minutes
Standing time:
5 minutes

1. Grease and line a 22 cm (8½ inch) square dish.
2. Mix together the flour, bicarbonate of soda, sugar, coconut and cocoa in a large bowl.
3. Place the margarine in a bowl and microwave on HIGH for 1 minute. Beat into the dry ingredients, with the eggs and milk, until smooth. Pour into the prepared dish.
4. Cook on HIGH for 8 minutes. Leave to stand for 5 minutes, then turn out onto a wire rack to cool.
5. Cut into squares to serve.

APPLE AND WALNUT LOAF

*175 g (6 oz) wholemeal
    flour
1 teaspoon baking powder
½ teaspoon mixed spice
75 g (3 oz) margarine
125 g (4 oz) light brown
    soft sugar
1 egg, beaten*

*250 g (8 oz) cooking
    apples, peeled and
    grated coarsely
50 g (2 oz) walnuts,
    chopped
3 tablespoons milk
25 g (1 oz) demerara
    sugar*

Makes 10 slices
Preparation time:
15 minutes
Power setting:
HIGH
Cooking time:
5 minutes
Standing time:
10 minutes

1. Place the flour, baking powder and mixed spice in a bowl, mix together and set aside.
2. Beat the margarine and light brown sugar together until creamy, then add the egg, beating well.
3. Fold in the flour mixture, then the apple and walnuts. Stir in the milk.
4. Turn the mixture into a greased 13 × 18 cm (5 × 7 inch) loaf dish, level the top, then sprinkle with the demerara.
5. Cook on HIGH for 5 minutes. Leave to stand for 10 minutes, then turn out onto a wire rack to cool. Cut into slices to serve. Best eaten same day as making.

INDEX

Photography by: Martin Brigdale
Designed by: Sue Storey
Home economist: Lorna Rhodes
Stylist: Liz Hippisley
Jacket photograph by: Paul Williams
Illustration by: Linda Smith
Typeset by Rowland Phototypesetting Ltd